TOM HENRICKSEN

Take your first steps into Vue.js

From basics and beyond

Contents

I

Basics of Vue.js

*In this first section we breakdown the basics of Vue.js.
This should get you up and running in no time. As
developers we enjoy getting our hands on the code.
We start installing things and then start learning
some of Vue.js biggest benefits. Let get coding!*

1

Get to know the basics of Vue.js

Photo by Joanna Kosinska on Unsplash

Last weekend I got to swing a hammer. I volunteered at Habitat for Humanity. It had been a while since I did work like this. I wasn't sure if I was a little rusty.

Another volunteer and I were cutting some boards. He said, "Do you want to cut this?" Initially, I was hesitant but, I jumped in and it all came back to me.

Transitioning to more front-end development I have picked up a few basics. Like a good carpenter, I want to know my tools. So I have been learning about the basics of Vue.js.

Vue.js

The website calls it, "The Progressive JavaScript Framework". So similar to other JavaScript frameworks like jQuery and Angular. Vue.js is reactive as well, like React. Sitepoint describes the difference this way:

> The main difference between Vue and React is that, while React is a JavaScript library used to build user interfaces, Vue is a JavaScript/TypeScript progressive framework for building web applications. "Progressive" means that its functionality and scope can easily be extended as a project grows.

In my time using it I have seen the power it has. There is a lot Vue.js can help you with as you create applications. Let's look next at what we can use it for.

Use options

If you have some static HTML you want to enhance Vue.js can do that. Or if you would like to add web components to your website. Vue.js allows you to create a Single-Page Application (SPA). Like the old desktop applications, it can constantly update the form.

Who uses

Developers want to know who uses something before they can be convinced. I can understand that level of scrutiny. Vue.js has quite a few major companies that use it.

This article outlines some major names that use it. Facebook, Netflix, and Adobe to name a few. When I see major names like this it makes me think it will be around for a while.

2

Installing Vue.js The Quick And Dirty Tips

Photo by Sigmund on Unsplash

Playing around with Vue.js couldn't be easier. You can jump in on the deep end of the pool by setting up your machine(more on that later). Or you can just play around in their playground. Or you could use JSFiddle too.

But First Node.js

Since having Node.js is required we first must check and see if your machine has it installed.

```
tomhenricksen@Toms-MacBook-Pro ~ % node -v
v16.13.1
```

Run the following command in your terminal: "node -v". Then you should see if you have a version installed or not. If not go here and download the LTS version to your machine.

Installing Node.js

You can double-click on the download and begin the installation. Once complete you can move on to the next part.

Application

Next, we can create an application from the command line. Run this command, "npm create vue@latest". Then accept the defaults like I did here.

```
tomhenricksen@Toms-MacBook-Pro ~ % npm create vue@latest
Need to install the following packages:
create-vue@3.8.0
Ok to proceed? (y)

Vue.js - The Progressive JavaScript Framework

  Project name:    vue-project
  Add TypeScript?         No   Yes
  Add JSX Support?        No   Yes
  Add Vue Router for Single Page Application development?   No   Yes
  Add Pinia for state management?        No   Yes
  Add Vitest for Unit Testing?      No   Yes
  Add an End-to-End Testing Solution?    No
  Add ESLint for code quality?        No   Yes

Scaffolding project in /Users/tomhenricksen/vue-project...

Done. Now run:

  cd vue-project
  npm install
  npm run dev

npm notice
npm notice New     version of npm available! 10.1.0 -> 10.2.4
npm notice Changelog: https://github.com/npm/cli/releases/tag/v10.2.4
npm notice Run npm install -g npm@10.2.4 to update!
```

Setting up Vue.js application

Then you can follow the directions laid out here to move into the
vue-project directory. Then install and run the dev environment.
You will see the following:

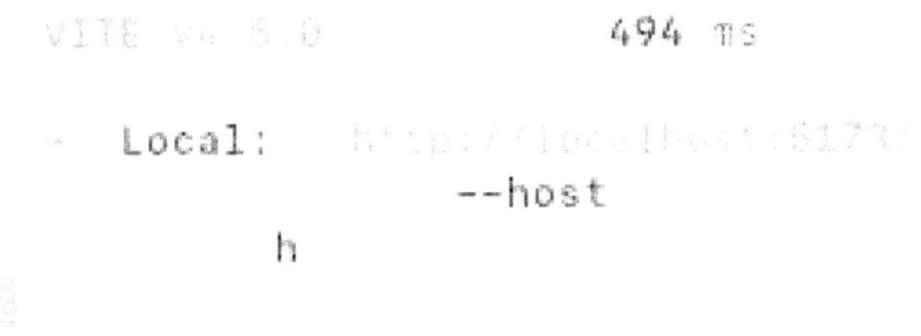

Running your local server

As it points out our server is running on http://localhost:5173/. If you go there you will see your Vue.js application running.

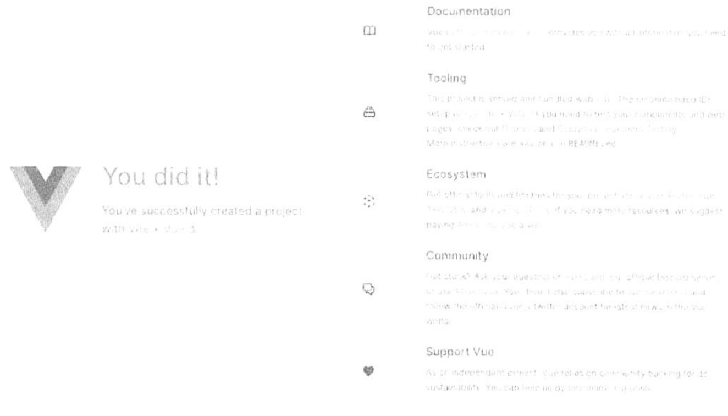

Now you are up and running. This was fairly easy. So to recap we have installed Node.js. This is used to run your Vue.js application. Then I created a basic application.

We were given a lot of options as we created this application. As your needs change you may need to look at each one of these. Some help with state management and others allow you to write unit tests for your code too.

You have taken a step into a larger world. Where will you go next?

3

Bind and render what? Know the basics of Vue.js

Photo by Michael Held on Unsplash

As an impatient learner, I skip over some fundamentals. I have learned to slow down and go thoroughly over them. Vue.js has some big changes from other JavaScript frameworks. Here are some of the basics you won't want to skim through.

Declarative Rendering

Vue applications have templates and script components. These enable the declarative renderings. In this example, we have a script section and a template section.

```
<script setup>
import { reactive, ref } from 'vue'
const counter = reactive({ count: 0 })
const message = ref('Declarative Rendering')
</script>

<template>
  <h1>{{ message }}</h1>
  <p>Count is: {{ counter.count }}</p>
</template>
```

Running this you will see the following in your browser:

Declarative Rendering

Count is: 0

Screenshot of code example

Note that we use reactive which makes the component change. Try this out on your own and see what you find. The best way to learn is to do it yourself!

Attribute Bindings

One of the big game-changers for Vue is dynamic binding. The v-bind is used quite often in Vue.js code. Let's see it in action.

```
<script setup>
import { ref } from 'vue'
const titleClass = ref('title')
</script>

<template>
  <h1 :class="titleClass">Shorthand</h1>
  <h2 v-bind:class="titleClass">using the v-bind
  prefix</h2>
</template>

<style>
.title {
  color: green;
}
</style>
```

In the first example, we use the shorthand abbreviation. In the second example, we use the regular syntax. You can use either. As you grow accustomed to it you will probably use the shorthand more.

Shorthand

using the v-bind prefix

Screenshot of code example

You should see this in your browser when you try to run this code on your local machine. Let's keep learning here.

Event Listeners

Another popular directive is v-on. This allows us to listen for events. Similar to the v-bind it also has a shorthand version.

```
<script setup>
import { ref } from 'vue'
const count = ref(0)
function counter() {
  count.value++
}
</script>
<template>
  Regular v-on directive:
  <button v-on:click="counter">count is: {{ count
```

```
  }}</button><br/><br/>
  Shorthand v-on directive:
  <button @click="counter">count is: {{ count
  }}</button>
</template>
```

In this example, we show you both kinds. Almost identical with a subtle twist for brevity. You will see both in the Vue.js code you see online.

Regular v-on directive: count is: 2

Shorthand v-on directive: count is: 2

Event Listener code example output

This is what you see in your browser if you test the code. Note that there is only one count value. Hopefully, you spotted that bug! It's not a big deal here but, it wouldn't work in code for work;)

We covered a few of the basics in Vue.js. From declarations, directives, and event listeners we are laying a foundation. Learn from my mistakes don't just read these examples, code them, and change them.

4

Forms, Lists, And So Much More In Vue.js

Photo by Mediamodifier on Unsplash

One of my first jobs working on the web was to take a paper form and create a webpage. It was quite a cumbersome process. The web technology wasn't as robust as it is now.

We are going to review some Vue.js tools that make forms easy. For instance, the two-way bindings are a wonderful tool to use. It's light years ahead of my early work in my career.

Form Bindings

Let's play around with two-way bindings. Check out this simple example using a v-model component.

```
<script setup>
import { ref } from 'vue'
const output = ref('')
</script>

<template>
  <h3>
    Two Way Bindings are fun!
  </h3>
  <input v-model="output" placeholder="Type here">
  <p>{{ output }}</p>
</template>
```

If we test it out you should see the text displayed on the screen as you type it.

Two Way Bindings are fun!

Can you see me now?

Can you see me now?

Two-way binding example output

If you don't see it check your code. I fat-fingered the name in the v-model at first. Mistakes happen but they are part of the learning!

Conditional Rendering

Developing code requires flexibility. We need to be able to execute code for one condition or the other. The if-then syntax is ubiquitous in programming. Vue.js has it too!

```
<script setup>
import { ref } from 'vue'
const love = ref(true)
function sheChangesHerMind() {
```

```
  love.value = !love.value
}
</script>
<template>
  <button @click="sheChangesHerMind">She changes her
  mind</button>
  <h1 v-if="love">She loves me!</h1>
  <h1 v-else>Not so much... </h1>
</template>
```

When dealing with fickle values we can use the v-if and v-else. Then your code can react to new input like in the example here.

When things go through the v-if you see this.

Screenshot of the v-if

When things go through the v-else you see this.

She changes her mind

Not so much...

Screenshot of v-else

No doubt you will get a chance to use these if you do some Vue.js programming.

List Rendering

Everyone has a list. Things to do, things to say. Here is how we render a list in Vue.js using the v-for syntax. As you can see it is great for looping over an array of objects.

```
<script setup>
import { ref } from 'vue'
// give each task a unique id
let id = 0
const newTask = ref('')
const tasks = ref([
  { id: id++, text: 'Wash dishes' },
  { id: id++, text: 'Sweep floor' },
  { id: id++, text: 'Vacuum bedroom' }
])
function addTask() {
```

```
  tasks.value.push({ id: id++, text: newTask.value })
  newTask.value = ''
}
function removeTask(task) {
  tasks.value = tasks.value.filter((t) => t !== task)
}
</script>
<template>
  <form @submit.prevent="addTask">
    <input v-model="newTask">
    <button>Add Task</button>
  </form>
  <ul>
    <li v-for="task in tasks" :key="task.id">
      {{ task.text }}
      <button @click="removeTask(task)">X</button>
    </li>
  </ul>
</template>
```

When you run this example you see this below.

Add Task

- Wash dishes X
- Sweep floor X
- Vacuum bedroom X

Screenshot of v-for example

Each of these simple exercises helps you understand how to become productive in Vue.js. Once you see how the basics work you can move quickly to more advanced topics.

Computed Property

To react to user input we can leverage computed properties. We could filter our task list to remove completed tasks. That would look something like this.

```
<script setup>
import { ref, computed } from 'vue'
let id = 0
const newTask = ref('')
const hideCompleted = ref(false)
```

```javascript
const tasks = ref([
  { id: id++, text: 'Wash dishes', done: true },
  { id: id++, text: 'Sweep floor', done: true },
  { id: id++, text: 'Vacuum floor', done: false }
])
const filteredTasks = computed(() => {
  return hideCompleted.value
    ? tasks.value.filter((t) => !t.done)
    : tasks.value
})
function addTask() {
  tasks.value.push({ id: id++, text: newTask.value,
  done: false })
  newTask.value = ''
}
function removeTask(task) {
  tasks.value = tasks.value.filter((t) => t !== task)
}
</script>
<template>
  <form @submit.prevent="addTask">
    <input v-model="newTask">
    <button>Add Task</button>
  </form>
  <ul>
    <li v-for="task in filteredTasks" :key="task.id">
      <input type="checkbox" v-model="task.done">
      <span :class="{ done: task.done }">{{ task.text
      }}</span>
      <button @click="removeTask(task)">X</button>
    </li>
  </ul>
  <button @click="hideCompleted = !hideCompleted">
    {{ hideCompleted ? 'Show all Task(s)' : 'Hide
    completed Task(s)' }}
  </button>
</template>
```

```
<style>
.done {
  text-decoration: line-through;
}
</style>
```

This builds on our previous work with the List Rendering. Computed properties will come in handy for your coding in Vue.js. I have used many of them in my short time programming front-end code.

Here is the first screenshot of this example, where all values are showing:

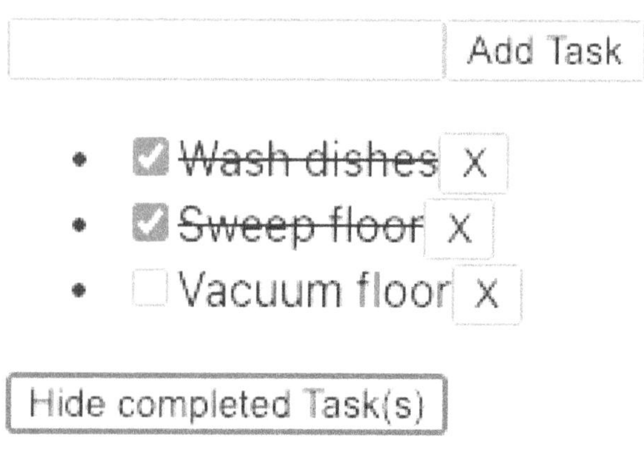

Screenshot of strikethrough

Here is one where you hide the completed tasks.

Screenshot of hiding tasks

There are numerous variations on this theme with computed properties. Depending on what your users ask for it can come in handy.

Overall, we have many tools to choose from when building applications with Vue.js. Of course, we just scratched the surface with these four items. As a coder, you will want to play around with these and use them too.

5

Circle of Life, get to know the Vue.js lifecycle

Photo by Joel & Jasmin Førestbird on Unsplash

Nothing lives forever. Perhaps you remember losing your first pet or a loved one. We all have a lifecycle. Vue.js also has it too.

Lifecycle

As we learn more we need to look under the hood. To do more internal changes on a page we must manipulate the DOM. That is where the Vue.js Lifecycle comes in.

Template Ref

First off, we need to request a reference to the template. To do that we use the following example.

```
<input ref="input">
```

To learn more about them and other types check out the documentation here.

Lifecycle Hooks

Vue.js exposes many lifecycle hooks to register callbacks. The one we will use today is onMounted. To see them all look at this diagram. As a newbie, this may be a bit overwhelming. Just know it's there.

```
<script setup>
import { ref, onMounted } from 'vue'
const pElementRef = ref(null)
onMounted(() => {
  pElementRef.value.textContent = 'Welcome to the
  Vue.js Lifecycle: onMounted has run'
```

```
})
</script>

<template>
  <p ref="pElementRef">text</p>
</template>
```

In this example, we use the onMounted hook. It is used to update the message.

Welcome to the Vue.js Lifecycle: onMounted has run

Screenshot of example code

This gives you an idea of how to start using the Lifecycle hook with the template ref.

Comes Alive

I reached out to a mentor about the Vue.js Lifecycle. This is what he had to say:

The vue lifecycle is the place to start! It's the way to understand how a vue component comes alive (and ultimately dies). While there's certainly a lot that happens between the arrows in the diagram, the hooks/methods available to us (they are the outlined red boxes as created, updated, destroyed, etc) are a useful guide to understanding when things happen, and what's available to the component at any given time.

So we need to get a firm grasp on this. That will help you see what is happening inside your application.

Composition of Components

He also mentioned we need to see how this relates to the components we use.

> *Understanding the basic composition of components and their use of data and events is probably a good way to see the lifecycle in action. The example code in that link shows "vanilla" vue, so while it looks different than what you'll find in the app, the app just has some syntactic sugar available. e.g. the prop binding like v-bind:title="post.title" in the blog example is nothing more than :title="title" in our app, or v-on:click="$emit('enlarge-text')" becomes @click="$emit('enlarge-text')"*

Essentially, if we see the big picture and the role each plays we can develop better solutions.

Don't hurry past the Vue.js Lifecycle. This is the plumbing we need to grasp. As you develop solutions you will have to dip into this. These hooks and references give you the power you need.

6

The pieces to the Vue.js puzzle

Photo by Ross Sneddon on Unsplash

Puzzles take patience. I have tried to put them together before. I cleared the table and put them out. Then it sits barely begun.

After walking by a few times I realize I should just put it away.

Crafting an application takes many pieces. We need to update some text after input. Or pass data or properties between components in our code. Today we will review some pieces in the Vue.js puzzle to help you do that.

Watchers

In life, we need to react to our surroundings. Software needs to do this too. The watch in Vue.js can perform this. In this example when a button is clicked we update information.

```
<script setup>
import { ref, watch } from 'vue'
const minionId = ref(1)
const minionData = ref(null)
async function fetchMinion() {
  minionData.value = null
  const res = await fetch(
    `https://jsonplaceholder.typicode.com/todos/${minionId.value}`
  )
  minionData.value = await res.json()
}
fetchMinion()
watch(minionId, fetchMinion)
</script>
<template>
  <p>"Don't worry, I will catch you."-Gru</p>
  <p>Minion id: {{ minionId }}</p>
  <button @click="minionId++"
  :disabled="!minionData">More Minons</button>
  <p v-if="!minionData">Loading...</p>
  <pre v-else>{{ minionData }}</pre>
</template>
```

Here is the code running in the browser. As we click the button the watcher code runs.

"Don't worry, I will catch you."-Gru

Minion id: 1

More Minons

```
{
  "userId": 1,
  "id": 1,
  "title": "delectus aut autem",
  "completed": false
}
```

Screenshot for example

Components

As an experienced, some might say old!, Java developer components remind me of objects. In Java, we might import an object, in Vue.js we import a component.

```
<script setup>
import Sub from './Sub.vue'
</script>
```

```
<template>
  <Sub />
</template>
```

This is the Main.vue that imports or calls the sub-component.

```
<template>
  <h2>A Sub Component!</h2>
</template>
```

This is the Sub.vue component. Note the syntax to call it in the Main.vue. These two are in the same folder. You may need to alter that depending on where you place the components.

A Sub Component!

Screenshot of the example

That is what you should see if you have everything working.

Props

When you have two components you may need to pass information. This can be done using props.

```
<script setup>
import { ref } from 'vue'
import ChildComp from './BabyBear.vue'
const greeting = ref('Mama Bear Loves you!')
</script>


<template>
  <ChildComp :msg="greeting" />
</template>
```

Here is our MamaBear.vue which is the parent component. It is passing the greeting.

```
<script setup>
const props = defineProps({
  msg: String
})
</script>


<template>
  <h2>{{ msg || 'Where are my props?' }}</h2>
</template>
```

BabyBear.vue receives the props message. Note we have a default message if the props aren't passed here. Also, the *defineProps()* is a compile-time macro that is automatically imported for you.

Mama Bear Loves you!

Screenshot of passing props

Your mileage may vary but your screenshot should match this one. Or at least be in the ballpark if you don't check the names and spelling of the props.

We have exposed you to some Vue.js puzzle pieces. I have shared some simple examples. Now you can take them and manipulate them. Use this as a jumping-in point.

7

And now the last bits of basics for Vue.js

Photo by Diane Picchiottino on Unsplash

The first programming I did with the Atari 400 was cumbersome. I worked through some examples to understand the BASIC programming language. Vue.js is easier to learn but has a broader API.

> *I had to spend countless hours, above and beyond the basic time, to try and perfect the fundamentals.*
>   *Julius Erving*

The time spent programming was enlightening. Each mistake in BASIC or Vue.js reveals new insights. Success or failure can help you down the road. Let's learn a little more in Vue.js.

Emits

Our sons' basketball practice never ended on time. So he would usually text us to pick him up. Likewise, child components need to notify the parent component. This is done through an *emit()* event.

```
<script setup>
import { ref } from 'vue'
import ChildComp from './ChildComp.vue'
const childMsg = ref('Not done yet.')
</script>

<template>
  <ChildComp @response="(msg) => childMsg = msg" />
  <p>{{ childMsg }}</p>
</template>
```

Here is the parent component. It is set to receive the *emit()* event from the child component.

```
<script setup>
const emit = defineEmits(['response'])
emit('response', 'We are done. Can you pick me up?')
</script>

<template>
  <h2>Son at basketball practice</h2>
</template>
```

This is our ChildComp.vue that sends the message "We are done. Can you pick me up?". This updates the *childMsg* on the Parent.vue.

Son at basketball practice

We are done. Can you pick me up?

Screenshot of the example

The simple example has the message updated on the parent component.

Slots

We have passed props and emit messages. If you want to pass template fragments you can use slots.

```
import { ref } from 'vue'
import MartianComp from './MartianComp.vue'
const msg = ref('take me to your leader!')
</script>

<template>
  <MartianComp>Martian Message: {{ msg
  }}</MartianComp>
</template>
```

In this main component, we use the MartianComponent. This our slot we can pass the code.

```
<template>
  <slot>Martian content</slot>
</template>
```

The MartianComp has the slot to receive the code. Emit and slots are similar tools. Depending on your use case experiment to see which one works best.

Progressive Framework

We have come a long way. Let's step back to review where Vue.js fits in the bigger picture. It is part of a larger ecosystem. Frontend development can be demanding, so you need to integrate other technologies.

Vue is designed to flex in many ways. As your stakeholders ask for changes you can adapt with it. With basic HTML and

JavaScript skills, you can harness the power of the web.

These last bits should help you see what you can do. The basics whet your appetite for future experiments. Create an application and try this out. Also, read some documentation to fill out your understanding.

8

Know the Vue Router Fundamentals

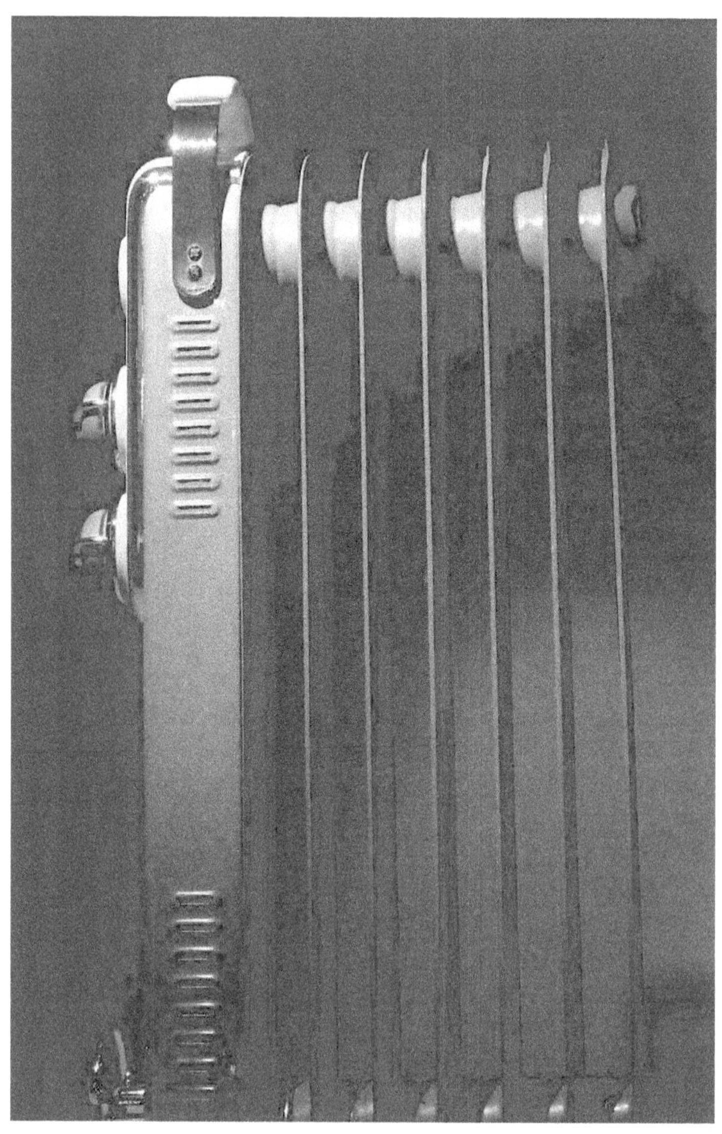

Photo by Anne Nygård on Unsplash

The Vue Router is like the air traffic control for your application. It tells everyone where they need to go. Any well-orchestrated software needs a process of how to work with input. Let's start with setting up the basics.

Setup

First thing we will install the vue-cli. You can do that with the following command.

```
npm install --save-dev @vue/cli-service
```

Then you should run the following command to add the router.

```
vue add router
```

You should see something like this.

```
tomhenricksen@Toms-MacBook-Pro vue-router % vue add router

    Installing @vue/cli-plugin-router...

up to date, audited 651 packages in 1s

86 packages are looking for funding
  run `npm fund` for details

4          severity vulnerabilities

To address all issues (including breaking changes), run:
  npm audit fix --force

Run `npm audit` for details.
    Successfully installed plugin: @vue/cli-plugin-router

? Use history mode for router?
  
    Invoking generator for @vue/cli-plugin-router...
    Installing additional dependencies...
```

Screenshot of adding a router

See the code

Looking at this folder in Visual Studio Code you would see the following items.

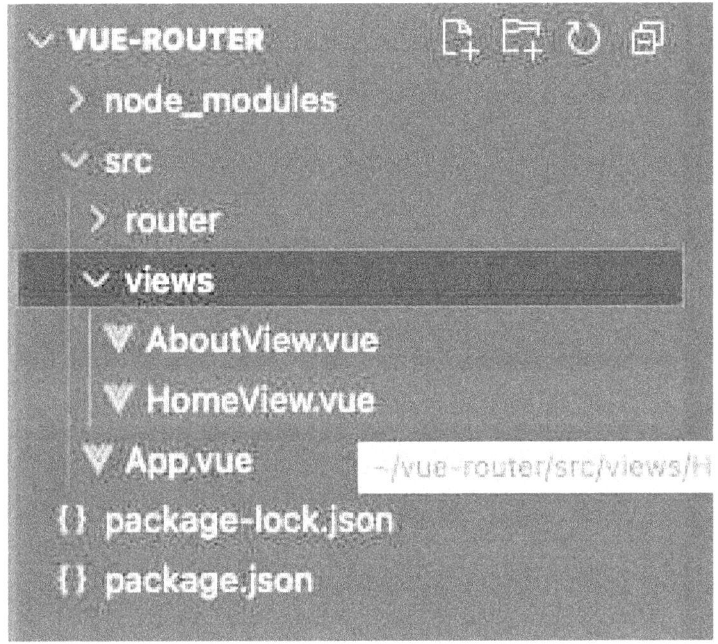

Screenshot of added folders

The router has created the views folder along with the AboutView.vue and HomeView.vue files. These are the pages and are referenced in the router/index.js.

```js
// src > router > JS index.js > ...
import Vue from 'vue'
import VueRouter from 'vue-router'
import HomeView from '../views/HomeView.vue'

Vue.use(VueRouter)

const routes = [
  {
    path: '/',
    name: 'home',
    component: HomeView
  },
  {
    path: '/about',
    name: 'about',
    // route level code-splitting
    // this generates a separate chunk (about.[hash].js) for this route
    // which is lazy-loaded when the route is visited.
    component: function () {
      return import(/* webpackChunkName: "about" */ '../views/AboutView.vue')
    }
  }
]

const router = new VueRouter({
  routes
})

export default router
```

Index.js file contents

This file has the router configuration. We import the VueRouter and then set up the routes in this file. Routes is an array of objects. Each one has a path, name, and component in the array.

Code Splitting

The About link uses code-splitting. This streamlines the assets the browser needs to download. Also, it improves the render times so it appears to be interactive instead of waiting to load files.

```
> ▼ App.vue > {} template
  <template>
    <div id="app">
      <nav>
        <router-link to="/">Home</router-link> |
        <router-link to="/about">About</router-link>
      </nav>
      <router-view/>
    </div>
  </template>
```

App.vue template section

In the App.vue we see the router link components. These tags are similar to an href but will not reload the page. This is part of the single-page application. This is a powerful feature that Vue.js applications offer and the router enables it.

The Vue Router does a lot for you. It creates the spine of your application. With this structure in place, you can begin to modify it to add what you need to achieve your outcomes. You can do this yourself or look at my code.

II

Vue.js Extras

Now you have some basics in your repertoire. Next, there are a few things you may want to use. Vuex helps you manage state. Then we show you Vuetify to make the User Interface look great. Lastly, we validate input with Vuelidate. You are not a Vue.js expert now but you have a good understanding to be productive.

Vuex Keeps Your Vue.js Components Under Control

Photo by Chris Leipelt on Unsplash

In the early days of web development, we dealt with stateless entities. My first web programs were JSP and Servlets. Each time we hit the server you had to ensure the users were authorized.

Today we have frameworks to handle that. State management is expected in any web framework. No one wants to go back to writing that code, I can assure you of that!

Vuex

As I learn more about the Vue.js world I see the need for state management. The components must coordinate information easily. Vuex is defined on its website as:

> Vuex is a state management pattern + library for Vue.js applications. It serves as a centralized store for all the components in an application, with rules ensuring that the state can only be mutated in a predictable fashion.

This makes it easier for developers to focus on solutions instead of worrying about basic plumbing. Let's clear up what we mean about this pattern.

State Management Pattern

Dipping our toe in the reactive world we run into state issues. The world of components needs to coordinate activity. According to AOE they define this as:

> State Management is a design pattern with the goal of efficiently sharing state data across components while separating domain representation from state management.

In the Vue.js world Vuex handles this orchestration. In comparison, the React world has Redux. This common challenge has to be handled by the framework.

Pinia

Pinia is the new version of the store library for Vue. It allows you to share state across components and pages. Pinia provides a timeline to track actions and mutations.

Install Vuex

You can start with the following line to install Vuex into existing Vue applications.

```
npm install vuex@next --save
```

This will install the correct version of Vuex and update the package.json file.

Create an index.js file inside the src/data folder.

```
import { createStore } from 'vuex'

export default createStore({

})
```

Then modify the main.js file to look like the following:

```
import { createApp } from 'vue'
import App from './App.vue'
```

```
import store from './store'

createApp(App).use(store).mount('#app')
```

This is bundling the store data for Vuex.

Then we can add the objects and values for the store.

```
import { createStore } from 'vuex'

export default createStore({
state: {
    firstName: 'John',
    lastName: 'Doe'
  },
mutations: {

},
actions: {

},
getters: {

}
})
```

This will get us ready for mutations, actions, and getters.

We can modify the App.vue to use the store.

```
<template>
  <div class="wrapper">
    <p>{{ $store.state.firstName }} {{
    $store.state.lastName }}</p>
    <div v-for="airport in airports"
    :key="airport.abbreviation">
```

```
      <airport-card :airport="airport" />
    </div>
  </div>
</template>
 ...
```

That should outline the basics to get Vuex installed. Check out the code used for this demonstration here.

In conclusion, State Management is required to keep things together. We talked about the basics of Vuex and how it fits in the Vue.js landscape. Pinia is the next iteration in the Vuex lifecycle. Then we reviewed the highlighted setting up Vuex. If you want to go deeper with Vuex check out this post from Adam Jahr.

10

I'm excited, Jumping into Vuetify, start with the components

Photo by Victor Rodriguez on Unsplash

I am sure it is no secret that developers are terrible designers.

It is no wonder that having User Input designers and User Experience people are required for a successful application.

That is where Vuetify can help. It gives the developers some help in crafting a quality interface. It works for Vue.js applications.

Vuetify

Their website says it succinctly:

> *Vuetify is a no design skills required Open Source UI Library with beautifully handcrafted Vue Components.*

This leads us to some of the benefits.

Benefits

It is free and open source. The components are moldable and pliable. There is extensive tooling and a vibrant community.

Play

You can easily play with it in Vuetify Play.

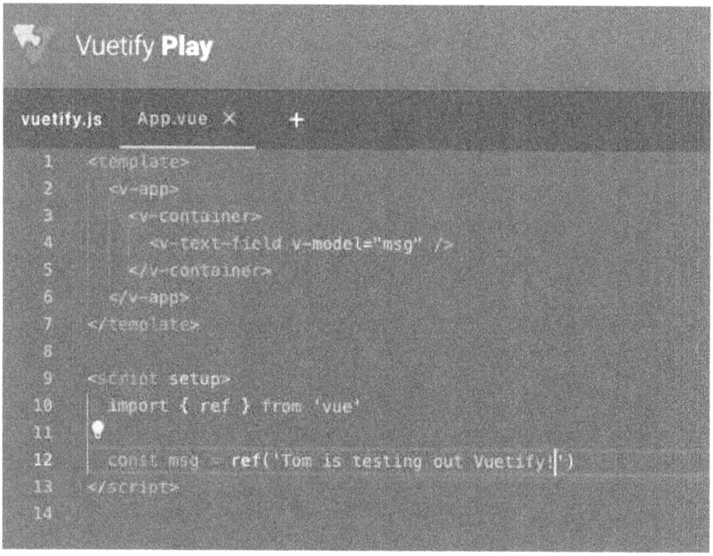

```
1   <template>
2     <v-app>
3       <v-container>
4         <v-text-field v-model="msg" />
5       </v-container>
6     </v-app>
7   </template>
8
9   <script setup>
10    import { ref } from 'vue'
11
12    const msg = ref('Tom is testing out Vuetify!')
13  </script>
14
```

Vuetify Play App.vue code screenshot

```
import { createVuetify } from 'vuetify'

export const vuetify = createVuetify({
  theme: {
    defaultTheme: 'light',
    //
  },
})
```

That is the vuetify.js file.

Vuetify Play Preview screenshot

It is easy and fun so try it yourself!

Create a Vuetify Application

Here are the steps to create a Vuetify application. Open a terminal and run the following command. **Note you may need to run this with sudo.**

```
vue create vuetify-demo
```

I ran this on my Mac and I saw the following.

```
Vue CLI v5.0.8
   Creating project in
 Initializing git repository...
 Installing CLI plugins. This might take a while...

              idealTree:default-gateway: fill            ROOT exec@1.0.
```

Starting the Vue install first.

Finishing the Vue install.

```
added 95 packages, and audited 972 packages in 6s

110 packages are looking for funding
  run `npm fund` for details

4           severity vulnerabilities

To address all issues (including breaking changes), run:
  npm audit fix --force

Run `npm audit` for details.
    Running completion hooks...

    Generating README.md...

    Successfully created project              .
    Get started with the following commands:

 $ cd vuetify-demo
 $ npm run serve
```

Once Vue is complete you need to add Vuetify. Here is the command to start that.

```
cd vuetify-demo
vue add vuetify
```

```
    Installing                          ...

added 10 packages, and audited 982 packages in 3s

111 packages are looking for funding
  run `npm fund` for details

4             severity vulnerabilities

To address all issues (including breaking changes), run:
  npm audit fix --force

Run `npm audit` for details.
  Successfully installed plugin:

  Choose a preset:
  Vuetify 2 - Configure Vue CLI (advanced)

  Vuetify 2 - Prototype (rapid development)
  Vuetify 3 - Vite (preview)
  Vuetify 3 - Vue CLI (preview)
```

I first saw an error taking the defaults. So I followed this advice and installed Vuetify 3 — Vue CLI.

```
  Choose a preset:
  Vuetify 2 - Configure Vue CLI (advanced)
  Vuetify 2 - Vue CLI (recommended)
  Vuetify 2 - Prototype (rapid development)
  Vuetify 3 - Vite (preview)
  Vuetify 3 - Vue CLI (preview)
```

Then it completed fine.

```
    Invoking generator for vue-cli-plugin-vuetify...
    Installing additional dependencies...


added 14 packages, and audited 996 packages in 5s

113 packages are looking for funding
  run `npm fund` for details

4        severity vulnerabilities

To address all issues (including breaking changes), run:
  npm audit fix --force

Run `npm audit` for details.
    Running completion hooks...

    Successfully invoked generator for plugin: vue-cli-plugin-vuetify
         Discord community: https://community.vuetifyjs.com
         Github: https://github.com/vuetifyjs/vuetify
         Support Vuetify: https://github.com/sponsors/johnleider
```

To test it out you should run the following command to start
your server.

```
npm run serve
```

Then hopefully you see this.

```
App running at:
- Local:   http://localhost:8080/
- Network: http://192.168.4.27:8080/

Note that the development build is not optimized.
To create a production build, run npm run build.
```

Then open your browser to localhost:8080 and check out your handy work!

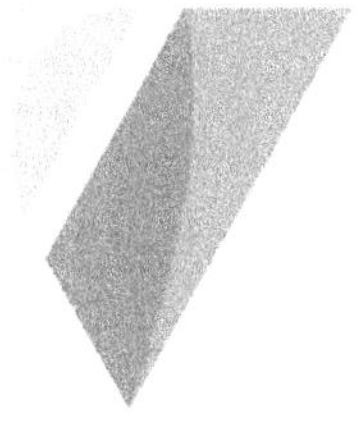

Jump In

Next, I would start to look at the components. There is a lot here to learn. Start with the basics. Try to create something basic and make a few mistakes. That is what learning is all about.

Vuetify has a lot to offer. If you are using Vue.js already then you should consider it for your layout. We shared how to play around with this. Then we created a simple application. The next step is up to you!

11

Vuelidate, Vue.js outstanding validation made jaw-droppingly easy

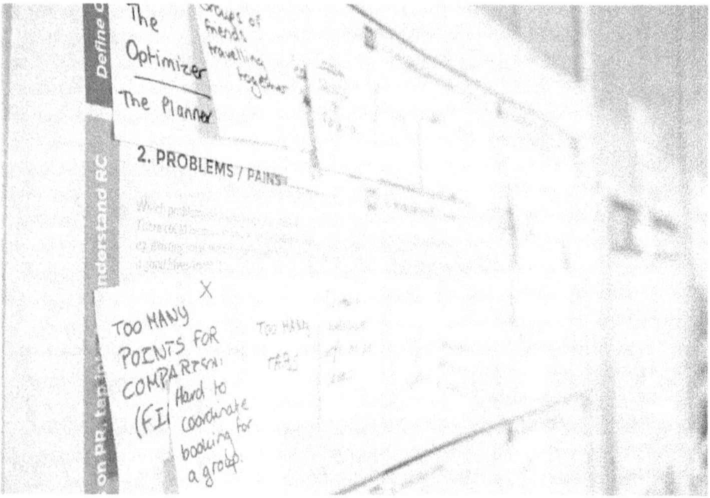

Photo by Daria Nepriakhina 🇺🇦 *on Unsplash*

I couldn't be more grateful when I began using a new framework like Vue.js and realized they have validation solutions. Vuelidate helps you check form input. No more reinventing the wheel.

Vuelidate

Vuelidate is a simple validation for Vue.js. It allows you to decouple it from the template. Vuelidate is dependency-free and uses a minimalistic design.

Install

Let's get started by setting up a basic Vue.js project. Enter the following on your command terminal. **Note you may need to run this with sudo.**

```
vue create vuelidate-demo
```

Select the default option to get things started.

```
Vue CLI v5.0.8
  Please pick a preset:
  Default (              )
  Manually select features
```

And keep rolling from there.

```
Vue CLI v5.0.8
    Creating project in
 Initializing git repository...
 Installing CLI plugins. This might take a while...

(                       ) ⠂ reify:acorn: timing
```

Finishing up you should see.

```
110 packages are looking for funding
  run `npm fund` for details

4           severity vulnerabilities

To address all issues (including breaking changes), run:
  npm audit fix --force

Run `npm audit` for details.
   Running completion hooks...

   Generating README.md...

   Successfully created project
   Get started with the following commands:

 $ cd vuelidate-demo
 $ npm run serve
```

Then check your install

If that looks good you can proceed. Type the following into your terminal command.

```
npm install @vuelidate/core @vuelidate/validators
```

Then you should see this.

```
added 4 packages, and audited 976 packages in 4s

111 packages are looking for funding
  run `npm fund` for details

4              severity vulnerabilities

To address all issues (including breaking changes), run:
  npm audit fix --force

Run `npm audit` for details.
```

Now you are ready to do some coding. So let's start with some basics.

Basics

Let's create a simple form that uses Vuelidate.

```
<template>
    Name:
    <label>
   <input v-model="name" @blur="v$.name.$touch">
   <div v-if="v$.name.$error">Name field has an
   error.</div>
</label>
</template>

<script>
import { useVuelidate } from '@vuelidate/core'
import { required } from '@vuelidate/validators'

export default {
  setup () {
    return {
      v$: useVuelidate()
    }
  },
  data () {
    return {
      name: ''
    }
  },
  validations () {
    return {
      name: { required }
    }
  }
```

```
}
</script>
```

Now when you open your browser you will see this. Prepare not to be amazed!

Name:

Name field has an error.

Wow! Aren't you impressed

We are using the *blur* event to call the touch method. This sets the *$dirty* state that Vuelidate monitors. This example also uses the *v-model* declaration that ties to the *$model* object. This is used to validate the object. Check out the code here.

Built-in Validators

There are numerous built-in validators. Use the following to include them.

```
import { required, maxLength } from
'@vuelidate/validators'
```

Required is a common one to use. Here is a code example.

```
export default {
  validations () {
    return {
      name: { required }
    }
  }
}
```

This will check for empty arrays or strings of whitespace. **Maxlength** checks for, you guessed it, the max length!

```
export default {
  validations () {
    return {
      name: {
        maxLength: maxLength(this.foo),
        maxLengthRef: maxLength(someRef),
        maxLengthValue: maxLength(10),
      }
    }
  }
}
```

It works on strings, objects, or arrays. There is a lot more to choose from. Also, you can write your custom validator if these don't solve your challenge.

Vuelidate is quite handy if you live in the Vue.js world. Validations can be quick and easy. With a little trial and error, you should find your way around in no time.

About the Author

Tom Henricksen is a problem-solving technology professional. He is a speaker and writer at Code is Easy. Starting from a developer he has worked as a Project Manager, Technical Lead, Scrum Master, and Manager of Software Development.

Tom has helped organizations with agile transformations. He has also coached and trained teams and individuals.

Tom has been an entrepreneur as well. He speaks and writes with a focus on technology roles. Tom was the founder of the Agile Online Summit and DevOps Online Summit. Where he led a strong online community of over 5,000 people.

Tom has learned how to solve challenging issues in technology and lead technical teams. He can help you develop those skills too!

You can connect with me on:

- 🌐 http://codeiseasy.co
- 🐦 https://twitter.com/TomHenricksen
- 🔗 https://www.linkedin.com/in/tomhenricksen

Subscribe to my newsletter:

- ✉ https://t.co/NkolrQgXHM